SODA BUTTE CREEK

SODA
BUTTE
FLATS

LAMAR RIVER

WHAT GOES ON INSIDE A
WOLF PACK

Follow the Adventures of a Wolf Family in Yellowstone National Park

Kathleen Yale *in partnership with the International Wolf Center*

Illustrated by Carrie Shryock

Storey Publishing

IT'S EARLY SPRING on the Northern Range of Yellowstone National Park, and a warm blanket of sunlight softens the sage-dotted landscape. Mountains rise in the distance. A winding river snakes through the valley.

Ground squirrels wake from their winter hibernation looking to fill their hungry bellies . . .

. . . while a ravenous badger tries to dig up pocket gophers.

An osprey soars overhead with a fresh catch.

A herd of female elk graze close together, and a small band of bison welcome the year's first red calf.

The resident wolf pack is on the move, scouting their territory.

THESE WOLVES, LIKE ALL WOLVES, ARE SOCIAL ANIMALS.
They like to live and travel in groups called packs. This medium-size pack is a family of eight wolves.

AAAAOOOO! WOOF!

Together they will hunt large prey, defend their territory, and take care of each other if someone gets hurt.

Mama and Papa are the leaders of the pack. Mama has a new litter of pups every year. In fact, she is pregnant now!

These three rambunctious yearling brothers were born last spring, and they are already the size of their parents.

GRRRRR!

GRUNT!

One has a star-shaped mark on his chest.

A trio of two-year-old siblings still lives with the pack. Most wolves in Yellowstone have either gray or black fur, but this sister has a very rare white coat.

It's an exciting time for the pack. Soon they will welcome their newest family members.

STATS: GRAY WOLF
(*Canis lupus*)

FEMALE

MALE

Average Weight:
Males 110 pounds (50 kg)
Females 90 pounds (40 kg)

Average Height:
Males 32 inches (81 cm)
Females 30 inches (77 cm)

Average Length:
71 inches (180 cm)

Eyes: Light yellow to brown or gold, excellent night vision

Nose: Probably can smell thousands of times better than you can!

Pack Size: Ranges from 3 to 35 wolves (the average in Yellowstone is around 11 wolves). The size of a wolf pack can change over the course of the year depending on how many pups are born, and whether animals leave the pack or die.

FUN FACT!
The heaviest male recorded in Yellowstone was nearly 150 pounds (68 kg)!

A LITTLE WAYS OFF FROM THE OTHERS, Mama paws at the ground. Her belly is bulging. She is pregnant and this is how she prepares her den.

SCRITCH
SCRATCH

As she digs, she flings dirt between her back legs.

Wolves often dig their dens into hillsides, below boulders, or under large tree roots like this one.

SNIFF!

She used this den site last year, so it is already in good shape—she's just freshening it up.

A good den site is secluded, close to fresh water, and not too close to another wolf pack's territory.

The narrow opening and entrance tunnel help keep out nosy bears and other possible predators.

This den has a simple design—just one chamber large enough for Mama to be able to lie down and move around a little.

Now that Mama is satisfied with the shape of her shelter, she starts to pull out tufts of fur from her belly. Exposing her skin will make it easier for her pups to nurse when they arrive.

ONE MORNING IN MID-APRIL, a week or so after she first started pawing at her den, Mama gives birth to three tiny pups.

It's cool and dark inside the den. Thick layers of earth muffle the sounds from the world above as she licks their soft, wet fur clean.

The pups crawl to her belly to nurse.

Each pup weighs only a single pound. They will be deaf and blind for a couple of weeks while their ears and eyes continue to develop.

The pups will spend the next several weeks here, safe underground, drinking their mother's milk and growing stronger every day.

While Mama stays around the den to care for the pups, the pack brings her food.

A few weeks later, the pups pop their fuzzy heads out of the den for the first time and sniff the spring air.

Oops! One takes a tumble and soon her siblings are piling on!

YAP! YAP!

Nearby, wildflowers like dainty spring beauties, glacier lilies, shooting stars, and steer's head are just opening.

BY LATE SPRING, the month-old pups are roly-poly balls of energy. They wrestle, pounce, and yap, but always stay within running distance of the den hole. Their parents, older siblings, and other pack mates take turns pupsitting.

YAP YAP!

YAP!

Sometimes a cheeky raven flaps down to tease the pups . . .

. . . until a watchful adult chases it away!

SQUAWK!

Papa has brought a curious toy home today. It looks very different from the bones and antler toys they've been gnawing on.

SNIFF

SNIFF

And oh! It feels different, too! Tiny teeth pierce holes in the crinkly plastic. Tugging and tossing the bottle around is fun!

CRUNCH!

GRRRRRRRRR...

Here comes their pale-coated big sister. The pups run toward her and dance around her paws, licking her muzzle, and begging for food.

WHIMPER WHIMPER!

The older wolf lowers her head and regurgitates some chewed-up meat on to the ground. The pups gobble it up eagerly.

ZZZZZZZZ

They are growing fast now and will gain about a pound a week over the next few months.

TOYS FOUND AT WOLF DENS

Adult wolves often bring home interesting sticks, bones, antlers, and even trash and other human-made objects for the pups to chew on.

THE PACK IS ENJOYING a lazy morning. One by one the wolves uncurl from their beds, stand up, and stretch forward in a deep bow. They raise their chests in a long back stretch. It's time to start the day.

The pups are eager to play and explore, but they are not quite ready to roam with the rest of the pack.

GRUNT!

A mountain bluebird hunts for insects.

FAMILIAR FLORA AND FAUNA

Spring welcomes back songbirds, delicate flowers, and the pollinators who drink their nectar. Other animals and plants, like ravens, foxes, and sagebrush, remain common year-round.

MOUNTAIN BLUEBIRD

WESTERN MEADOWLARK

RAVEN

SILVERY BLUE MOTH

YAP!

A red fox yaps in the distance.

The pack heads out to roam their territory and look for prey.

WHINE!

The black pup tries to follow the pack as they leave, but her older sister leads her back to the den.

A western meadowlark sings out from its perch in the sagebrush.

RED FOX

SAGEBRUSH

ARROWLEAF BALSAMROOT

STICKY GERANIUM

DOUGLAS FIR

AS THE SUN REACHES HIGH OVERHEAD, the pack finally has some luck. They sniff prey in the wind and, trotting over a ridge, spot a small herd of elk.

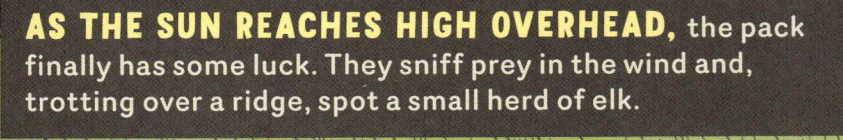

They lower their heads and barrel toward their prey. At a full sprint, a wolf can run about 35 miles (56 kilometers) per hour, a close match to an elk's speed.

Most of the herd is soon out of range, but a few wolves are on the heels of a bull elk.

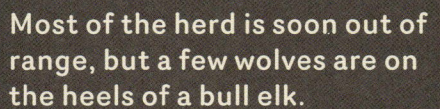

Suddenly the bull stops running and turns to face his pursuers.

Although he dropped last year's antlers in late winter, his new rack is growing fast. He looks powerful. The wolves won't attack him if he stands his ground.

This eager yearling makes a lunge from behind.

He gets a glancing kick to the chest. Wolves can die from such blows, but he'll be okay this time. Lesson learned.

YIP!

GRUNT!

WHINE!

Hunting can be hard, and it's often unsuccessful. The pack goes hungry for now but they're used to it. Wolves often go for several days with no food.

ELK

Elk are the most abundant hooved animal (or ungulate) in Yellowstone. They make up an important part of a wolf pack's winter diet, and their bodies are a key food source for bears, cougars, coyotes, bald eagles, and other scavengers.

Only bulls grow branched antlers, which they shed in spring and regrow each year.

BULL: Average 700 pounds (318 kg), about 5 feet high at the shoulder

COW: About 500 pounds (227 kg)

CALF: About 30 pounds (14 kg) at birth, born with pale spots that fade with age

NOW THAT THE PUPS are spending more time out of the den, it's time for them to learn how to be proper wolves and follow the pack's rules.

Mama reminds everyone she is the pack leader by standing up straight, raising her tail high, and perking up her ears. Her yearlings keep their tails lowered.

The key to getting along in any group is good communication. The pups watch Mama playing with their older brother.

If her family isn't listening, she might curl up her lip to show some teeth.

GRRRRRRRRR

To show he understands, the yearling tucks his tail, lowers his ears, and licks her nose. He may crouch low to the ground or roll over and show his belly, too.

The pups play, too, wagging their tails and dancing around. The black yearling playfully bows his front legs.

The pack also uses sound to share information. Barks are warnings that danger is near.

RUFF RUFF!

WHIMPER

Whimpering means "I'm in pain" or "I won't fight."

Growls mean "Stay away."

GRRRRR!

AAOO OOOO

Howls are used to communicate over long distances.

AAAAYAAA HOOOOOO

Defensive howls warn other packs to stay away, and social howls are used to say, "Hey! I'm over here!" or just "Woo hoo! It's fun to howl together!" The pups add their own high-pitched howls to their family's low musical cries.

AAAROOOOOOOO

IT'S DUSK IN EARLY JULY. Shadows stretch long as the air cools, and the sky blushes from pink to velvety purple.

At about three months old now, the pups' blue eyes have turned a golden yellow.

As the pack rallies and readies to move, the pups join in the excitement, yipping and howling with the others.

Papa starts leading the pack away, and this time no pupsitter holds the pups back. They fit right into the family line of wolves. Farewell, den! See you again next year. Next stop: a new homesite.

The journey isn't long, just a mile or so. For the pups, it's a grand adventure full of new sounds and strange smells.

HOO-H'HOO-HOO-HOOO

SNIFF SNIFF

But the cool, clear water tastes the same when they stop for a needed break!

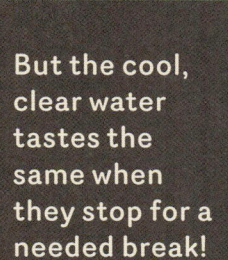

At last, the pack arrives at a familiar destination.

UP ALL NIGHT

Wolves are crepuscular animals, which means they are mostly out and about at dawn and dusk, although they could be active at any time of day or night. Diurnal animals are active during the day and rest at night. Nocturnal animals, like the ones pictured below, are active at night and sleep most of the day.

GREAT HORNED OWL

PORCUPINE

LITTLE BROWN BAT

WESTERN TOAD

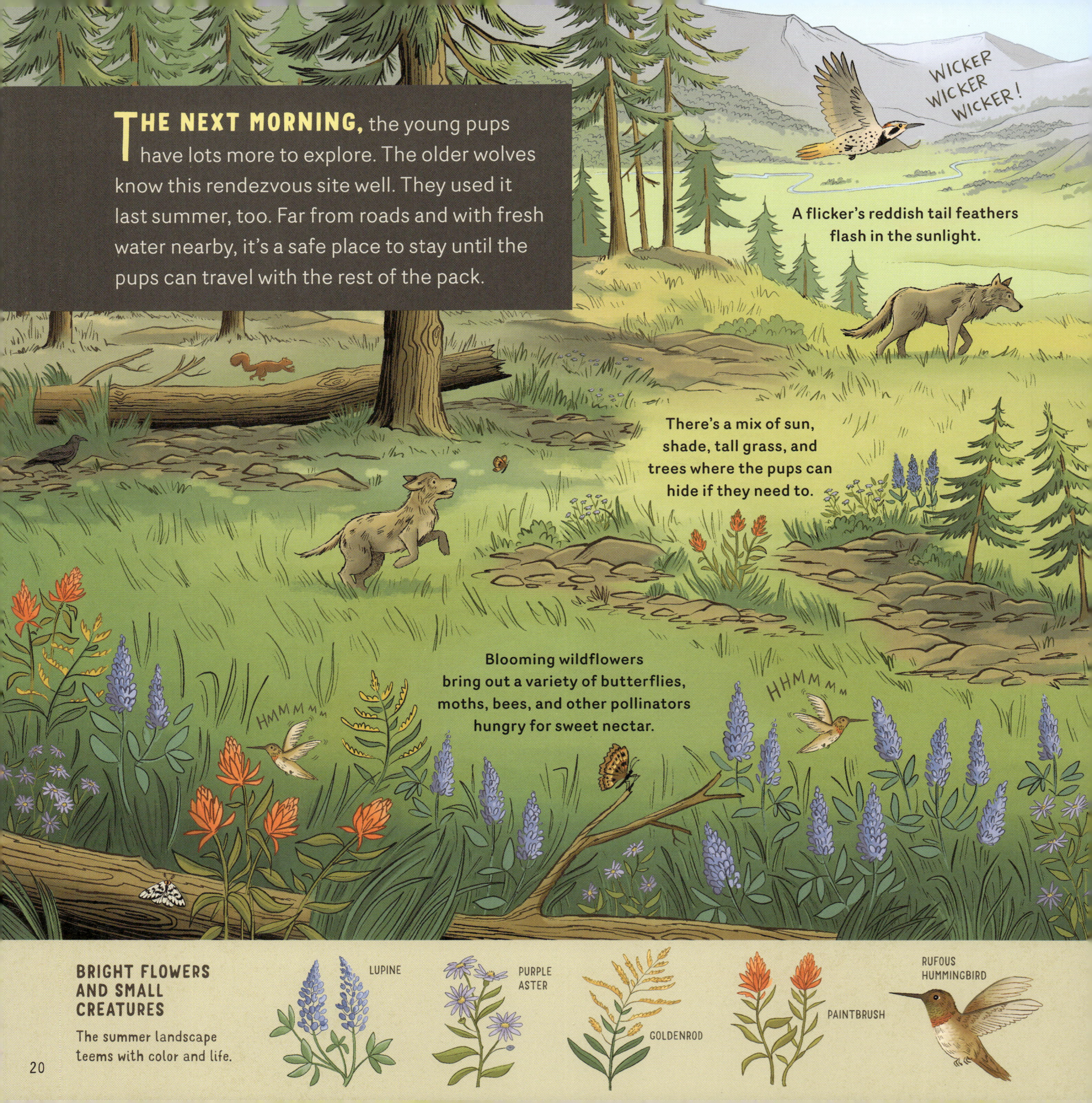

WICKER WICKER WICKER!

THE NEXT MORNING, the young pups have lots more to explore. The older wolves know this rendezvous site well. They used it last summer, too. Far from roads and with fresh water nearby, it's a safe place to stay until the pups can travel with the rest of the pack.

A flicker's reddish tail feathers flash in the sunlight.

There's a mix of sun, shade, tall grass, and trees where the pups can hide if they need to.

Blooming wildflowers bring out a variety of butterflies, moths, bees, and other pollinators hungry for sweet nectar.

HMMMmm

HHMMMm

BRIGHT FLOWERS AND SMALL CREATURES

The summer landscape teems with color and life.

LUPINE

PURPLE ASTER

GOLDENROD

PAINTBRUSH

RUFOUS HUMMINGBIRD

ROOOARRR!

RAT-TAT-TAT!

Across the hills, loud bellows ring out from a small herd of bison. Two bulls charge and bash their heads together, competing for the cows' attention.

RUFFFF!

TEEEEEE!

Not everyone is happy about their new neighbors!

DOWNY WOODPECKER

NORTHERN FLICKER

HERA BUCKMOTH

MILBERT'S TORTOISESHELL BUTTERFLY

GOLDEN-MANTLED GROUND SQUIRREL

RED SQUIRREL

TONIGHT, most of the adults are on the move. Under a dome of bright stars, they roam the boundaries of their territory. Every so often, someone stops to pee or poop. This is a kind of chemical messaging called scent-marking.

It's how they keep tabs on what goes on in their home range. It lets other wolves moving through the area know this spot is already occupied by a pack—a pack that will protect and defend its territory.

Mama and Papa scent-mark the most. They both raise a back leg when urinating. This reminds everyone they are in charge of the pack.

The other females squat to pee, while the males stand and lean forward.

Mama kicks up some dirt for good measure. Like all wolves, she has special glands on her tail, genitals, and between her toes. These glands brew body chemicals called pheromones that give off a particular smell.

SCRITCH

SCRAA AATCH

She scrapes her paws across the ground to help spread her scent and leave a message that says, "I was here."

Wolves can recognize and distinguish the scent of a packmate from that of an unknown wolf just by sniffing out these scent marks.

SNIFF SNIFF

SNIFF SNIFF

And lo and behold, the black yearling is on the trail of an unfamiliar smell.

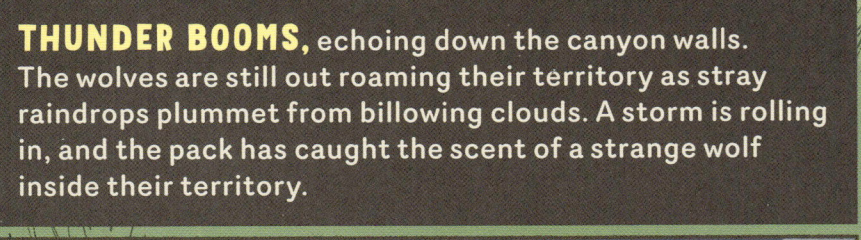

BOOOOM!!

THUNDER BOOMS, echoing down the canyon walls. The wolves are still out roaming their territory as stray raindrops plummet from billowing clouds. A storm is rolling in, and the pack has caught the scent of a strange wolf inside their territory.

SNIFF SNIFF SNIFF

RUFF! RUFF RUFFFF!!!

Wind whips at their fur as they follow the smell down a gully and find a rival pack in the distance.

The two packs howl back and forth, listening for who has greater numbers. Will they fight?

AAAARRROOOOOOOOO
AAAAAAAOOOOAAA

A bright bolt of lightning slashes the sky. In a flash, the pack is racing toward the invaders.

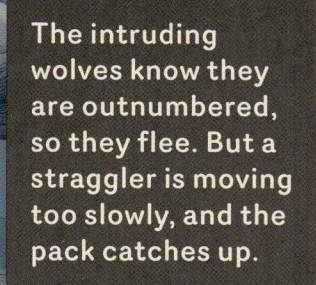

The intruding wolves know they are outnumbered, so they flee. But a straggler is moving too slowly, and the pack catches up.

GGRRROOWWLL

They surround him, snarling. The stray wolf rolls onto his belly as Mama and Papa tower over him.

GRRRRRR...

Clashes like these often turn deadly, but today, after some snarling and biting, they let the interloper go. He runs off limping while the pack howls in triumph.

AAAROOOOOOOO

AAAAAHHHOOOOOOOOOO
AAAAHHWWWOOOOOO

Clouds burst and a heavy rain falls. But the pack doesn't seem to mind. Their howling can be heard for miles, as they let everyone know they have successfully defended their territory.

IT'S BEEN ABOUT SIX MONTHS since the pups were born. They have grown a lot in that time and are finally ready to leave the rendezvous site.

From now on the pups will stay with the rest of the pack as they move through their territory, following interesting smells and hunting for their next meal.

Along the riverbank the pups trot past alder and willow bushes full of cheerful birdsong. They sniff beaver-chewed sticks and fresh elk tracks pressed into the mud.

WHIT!

TINK! TINK! TINK!

QUACK!
QUACK!
QUACK!

Without predators, elk herds can grow large, eating more and more of these plants that birds and other animals depend on. By hunting elk, wolves help keep this ecosystem in balance.

Eventually Papa finds a good place to cross and plunges in. The water is shallow here and slower moving.

The gray pup is nervous to cross her first river. She pauses and looks to Mama, watching where she steps.

WHINE

She stumbles a little and . . . eeek! Cold water splashes up her nose.

SPLASH!

But soon Mama is at her side. She encourages the pup as she half walks, half swims to the other side.

RIPARIAN ZONES

Areas where freshwater meets land, like riverbanks, lakeshores, and wetlands, provide important habitats for all sorts of different plants and wildlife.

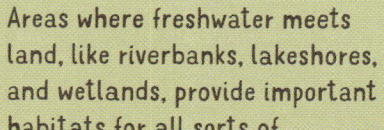

YELLOW WARBLER

WILLOW FLYCATCHER

GREAT BLUE HERON

BELTED KINGFISHER

BEAVER

YELLOWSTONE CUTTHROAT TROUT

COLUMBIA SPOTTED FROG

KEE-EEEE-ARR!

NOW AUTUMN'S SOFT SUNLIGHT filters through yellowing aspen and cottonwood leaves, tinting everything a brilliant gold. A chill is in the air, and the wolves' fur is getting thicker.

Osprey, red-tailed hawks, and golden eagles pepper the sky, soaring along thermal columns of rising air.

The wolves nap, gathering their energy for the next hunt.

EEEEU EEEEU EE EEU!

Silvery-green sagebrush gives off a pungent earthy smell.

SUMMER INTO FALL

The days are cooler now, and a new energy fills the landscape. Leaves fall, seasonal birds depart, and mammals eat as much as they can to fatten up before winter.

COTTONWOOD

WILLOW

RABBITBRUSH

BOHEMIAN WAXWING

MALLARD

HONK!
HONK!
HONK!

Overhead a large, ragged V of Canada geese honks its way across the clouds, heading south.

Pronghorns are Yellowstone's smallest ungulate. Both does and bucks have horns.

OHHH EEEEEEEE!

An eerie, high-pitched screech pierces the afternoon calm. Bull elk are bugling! They call out to possible mates, hoping to impress them with their massive antlers.

CANADA GOOSE

RED-TAILED HAWK

GOLDEN EAGLE

BISON

PRONGHORN ANTELOPE

KRAAAA!

ONE PALE DAWN, the sun rises over a riotous scene. Last night's hunt was successful! Now the wolves swarm around the body of their kill.

Mama and Papa dig in, racing to gobble up the elk's nutritious heart, liver, and kidneys.

The other wolves jostle for space, ripping off chunks of meat with their sharp teeth.

SNARRRLLL!

AH AH AH AH!!

WOOF!

This yearling keeps watch over a flurry of ravens and magpies, occasionally chasing them away. The birds will get their turn eventually.

The pack doesn't get to eat every day, so when they do get a meal, they feast. A big elk like this old bull provides enough food for everyone in the pack to eat their fill.

Having gorged themselves, they lie around with big, full bellies.

Speaking of scavenging . . . uh-oh! Here comes trouble. A big old grizzly bear waddles into the kill site. The pack jumps up in alarm.

They growl and lunge at him. Papa even nips him on the butt!

Grizzly and black bears are omnivores, meaning they eat both plants and meat. Most of their meat comes from scavenged carrion, but they also hunt young elk and deer in the early summer.

Black bears aren't just black. They come in various shades of brown, cinnamon, and even blond, so coloration is not a solid way to tell them apart from grizzlies.

dish face profile — small, rounded ears — shoulder hump

Grizzly Bear

long claws

straight face profile — tall ears — no shoulder hump

Black Bear

shorter claws

But it's no use. Grizzly bears usually get what they want, and this one wants breakfast!

WHINE WHIMPER

The wolves are resigned and wander off to nap somewhere nearby where they can keep an eye on the bear in case he leaves.

Meanwhile the grizzly digs into his free meal.

This bear is an eating machine. He is trying to fatten up as much as possible before a long winter hibernation, when he won't eat or drink for months.

ZZZZZZZZZZZZZZZ

THE NEXT DAY, the grizzly has moved on in search of more food, but the kill site is still bustling with activity.

A bald eagle tears scraps off a bone with her sharp, hooked beak.

Ravens scrounge the ground for leftovers, their dark, iridescent feathers shining. Feisty magpies wait their turn.

A cautious coyote slinks in, snags another leg bone, and trots off to gnaw on it in secret. A whole ecosystem of scavengers has benefited from the wolves' hunt.

CROAK!

WOLVES AND RAVENS
An Unlikely Pair

Ravens and wolves are highly intelligent, social animals who share a special relationship.

Ravens follow wolves while they hunt, then wait for a chance to steal food. On occasion, wolves may benefit from watching the birds and following them to new food sources.

And their relationship isn't just about food—they've been known to playfully chase each other. Biologists have even seen the birds pulling on wolves' tails!

prominent curved beak

feather bristles

Raven

shaggy throat feathers

wedge-shaped tail

OVERNIGHT, as the wolves are resting, a fierce wind gusts in from the north and heavy snow begins to pile up. The winter season is harsh, and species who do not migrate or hibernate need special adaptations to survive the cold.

Ruffed grouse dive into fluffy snowbanks to keep warm. Ducks have special arteries and veins in their feet to avoid freezing. Beavers hole up in their snug lodges to stay out of the wind.

But the wolves get along well in winter and are perfectly cozy in their thick winter coats.

Long outer guard hairs protect them from wind and water, and a dense layer of underfur insulates them from the cold. It's a vicious −35°F (−37°C) today, and they don't mind a bit!

Winter can make it easier for wolves to hunt. Their wide paws allow them to walk across snow without sinking down as far as their prey.

The wolves get on the track of some elk, who are worn out from walking through the deep snow and weak from lack of food.

Elk leave parallel lines as they drag their hooves through snow.

The pack trots on, disappearing into the snow. Perhaps they will get lucky with an easy hunt.

MASTERS OF DISGUISE

Snowshoe hares, white-tailed jackrabbits, and short- and long-tailed weasels have a special trick to survive in the snow: seasonal camouflage! Their normally brown coats turn mostly white in winter. This adaptation helps them hide in the snow and evade predators or sneak up on prey.

SNOWSHOE HARE

WHITE-TAILED JACKRABBIT

LONG-TAILED WEASEL

NOT ALL WINTER DAYS are so brutal. Today it's dazzlingly bright. The sunlight reflects off the frost and makes every tree, branch, rock, and snowdrift sparkle and shine.

GRRRR...

RUFF! RUFF!

The wolves are in a playful mood, pawing, prancing, and wrestling around.

The pups are still growing, but more slowly now. Although they're as big as their older siblings, they aren't fully mature yet.

Birds leave feather prints like little snow angels.

TRACKS IN THE SNOW

Tracks reveal which animals are in the area, if they are traveling alone or in a group, and where they are headed.

MOOSE

OTTER

CHEE CHEE
DZEE DZEE!

TSEE
TSEE!

Chickadees and golden-crowned kinglets hop between treetops.

WOOF!

Animal tracks crisscross across the landscape.

UH UH UH!

Farther down the riverbank, a family of otters bounds up a snowdrift and belly-slides into the water.

This one just caught a fish!

COYOTE

PINE MARTEN

MOUNTAIN CHICKADEE

GOLDEN-CROWNED KINGLET

IT'S FEBRUARY NOW, and love is in the air. Mama and Papa are spending more time alone together. They're being extra affectionate and flirty . . . touching noses, bumping into each other, walking closely side by side.

HUFF HUFF!

SNUFF!

They flirt by mouthing each other's muzzles, gently nipping fur, and resting their heads and draping front paws over each other's necks.

They double-scent mark, which means when one pees, the other immediately pees on the same spot.

And for days they have been sleeping curled up next to each other.

Raven pairs are feeling extra lovey, too. They circle each other in the air, diving and rolling, and even lock talons together in midflight.

KRAAA! KRAAA!

Resting from their aerial acrobatics, they perch wing to wing, gently preening each other's shaggy neck feathers.

This is called courtship behavior. It means the wolves are ready to mate and have more pups, and the ravens will start rebuilding their giant stick nests.

After they mate it will be about two months before Mama gives birth to her new litter of pups. But ravens' eggs will hatch in just three weeks.

TWO OF A KIND

Wolf pairs often, but not always, stay together to rear their pups and lead the pack until one partner dies. Yellowstone is home to other animals who stick by their mates to raise their young, including these:

SANDHILL CRANES

BALD EAGLES

BEAVERS

COYOTES

THE RIVERS RUSH AND CREEKS SWELL WITH SNOWMELT.

Everyone knows new pups are on the way. With nearly a dozen wolves in the pack, it's feeling a little crowded. The black yearling, who is now about two years old, is antsy. He'd like the chance to lead his own pack.

So one day, he slips away and sets out on a journey.

After several days of wandering, he finds a nice gap between pack territories. There is prey here, and water nearby.

He marks his new territory, hoping to catch the interest of a potential mate.

It works! Finally, a lone female approaches. She moves cautiously, keeping her head up and back straight.

He dances forward, wagging his tail nervously.

They sniff each other and jump back. It's tense for a moment. Will they like each other?

A few minutes later they're playfully prancing back and forth. The match is good.

The pair will stick together and start a new family of their own.

MEANWHILE, something exciting is happening back in the pack's territory. A few hours ago, a cougar brought down a mule deer. She ate her fill and is now caching the rest of her prey to eat later, covering it with grass, twigs, and dirt.

Unfortunately for her, the wolves have sniffed out this free meal.

As the pack rushes in, the cougar bolts up a nearby tree. She's incredibly strong, and her long, sharp claws dig into the rough bark.

WOOF!

She may be fierce, but she does not want to tangle with a wolf pack. The cougar watches from above as the wolves devour the rest of her hard-won kill.

At least she filled her belly once. She's pregnant and needs all the food she can get to help the kittens inside her grow.

HISSSSSSS

But the wolves need to eat, too, especially Mama, who has her own babies on the way. Like all of Yellowstone's predators, they will hunt, scavenge, or steal whatever food they can to stay fit and healthy.

When the carcass is only bones and hide, the pack wanders off.

The cougar stays tucked away until nightfall, when the wolves are long gone and it's safe to come down. Both mamas will soon head underground to give birth in the safety of their dens.

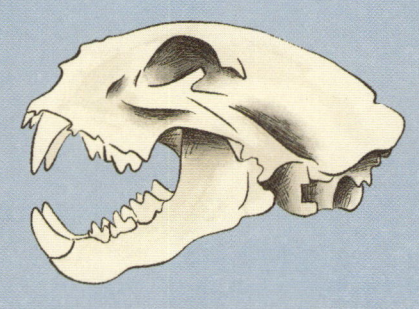
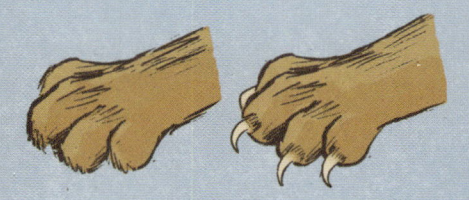

A CHORUS OF BIRDS rings out over the land. It's a glorious spring day, and the plateau is bustling with new life.

Elk herds welcome spotted, gangly-legged new calves. Bison calves play near their mothers.

The migratory birds are returning. Red-winged blackbirds, meadowlarks, bluebirds, and kinglets gather nesting materials.

CONK-LA-REE!

A mother black bear nurses her cubs.

And who's this? Mama has given birth to a new litter. Four new wolf pups scamper out of their den, ready to greet the day, the season, the park, and their new life.

RIEKA

BLACKSTONE

From the International Wolf Center

Now that you've read this book, you know a little more about wolves and how they live and work together in family groups called packs. You've also learned about the important role they play in Yellowstone National Park and ecosystems around the world! Wolves can be found not only in North America, but also in Europe, Asia, and the Middle East.

The Return of the Howl

Wolves once lived across most of North America. They coexisted with local Indigenous communities until the arrival of European colonists who saw wolves as a threat to their livestock and settlements. Aggressive poisoning and hunting campaigns caused wolf populations to drop rapidly throughout the United States. By the mid-1900s, wolves were gone from most of the lower 48 states.

In 1967, gray wolves were placed on the endangered species list, and their populations began to rebound in places like Minnesota, Wisconsin, and Michigan. In 1995, wolves were reintroduced into Yellowstone National Park, as well as the mountains of Idaho. Their populations began to recover in western states.

Other reintroduction efforts have since taken place in Arizona, New Mexico, North Carolina (red wolves), and most recently Colorado. Today there are more than 7,500 wolves in the lower 48 states along with tens of thousands more in Canada and Alaska. The howls are back!

CAZ

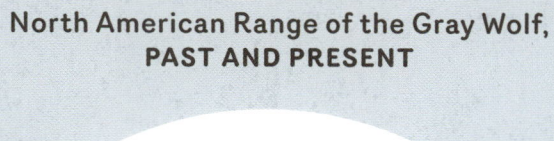

**North American Range of the Gray Wolf,
PAST AND PRESENT**

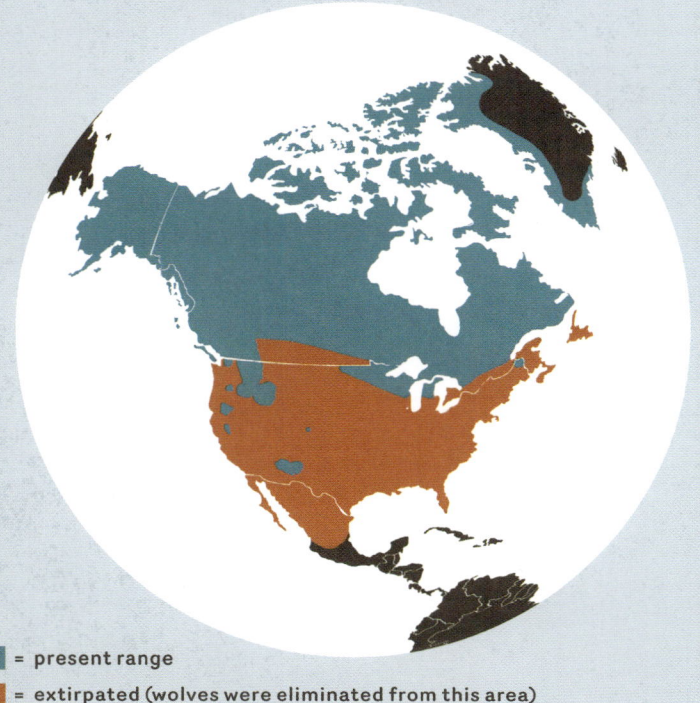

■ = present range

■ = extirpated (wolves were eliminated from this area)

GRAYSON

How Can I Help Wolves?

Everyone can help wolves by learning the facts and spreading the word about why they are such amazing animals and how important they are to the ecosystems in which they live.

LEARN MORE: Visit websites, watch documentaries, and read books about wolves. There's so much to discover! A great place to start is on the International Wolf Center website, wolf.org

SPREAD THE WORD: Tell your friends and family about wolves and why you like them!

BE WOLF AWARE: If you live where wolves live, be respectful and keep your distance. Always keep your pets on a leash. Don't leave food outside where it will attract wild animals.

What Is the International Wolf Center?

The International Wolf Center is a wolf education facility located in the heart of wolf range in Ely, Minnesota. It was founded by famed researcher Dr. L. David Mech, who has studied wolves around the world for more than six decades. The International Wolf Center includes exhibits on wolves and wolf research, a classroom, a theater, and a gift store. The stars of the Center are a pack of ambassador wolves who live in a large, tree-filled enclosure.

The Center produces a wide variety of educational content and programming about wolves. Learn more about wolves and check out the ambassador wolf webcams at wolf.org, or follow the International Wolf Center on Facebook or Instagram.

For all the wolf advocates, researchers, and enthusiasts out there, and for the dynamic beasts themselves.

With thanks to Dave Mech, Grant Spickelmier, and the International Wolf Center, and gratitude for Daniel Stahler and everyone at the Yellowstone Wolf Project, past and present.

And a special *Ayoooah!* to Wendy and Richard Pini for fueling my young obsession with wolves. —K. Y.

The mission of Storey Publishing is to serve our customers by publishing practical information that encourages personal independence in harmony with the environment.

Edited by Hannah Fries
Art direction and book design by Jessica Armstrong
Illustrations by © 2025 by Carrie Shryock
Photography by Abby Keller, 46 (Rieka and Blackstone); International Wolf Center, 46 (Caz), 47 (Grayson)

Text © 2025 by Kathleen Joan Yale
From the International Wolf Center text
© by International Wolf Center

Storey Publishing
210 MASS MoCA Way
North Adams, MA 01247
storey.com

Storey Publishing is an imprint of Workman Publishing, a division of Hachette Book Group, Inc., 1290 Avenue of the Americas, New York, NY 10104. The Storey Publishing name and logo are registered trademarks of Hachette Book Group, Inc.

Distributed in Europe by Hachette Livre, 58 rue Jean Bleuzen, 92 178 Vanves Cedex, France

Distributed in the United Kingdom by Hachette UK Ltd., Carmelite House, 50 Victoria Embankment, London EC4Y 0DZ

ISBNs: 978-1-63586-850-0 (paper over board); 978-1-63586-851-7 (ebook)

Printed in China through Asia Pacific Offset on paper from responsible sources

10 9 8 7 6 5 4 3 2 1

APO

Library of Congress Cataloging-in-Publication Data on file

Can you find these plants and animals in this book?

RABBITBRUSH

DOUGLAS FIR

WESTERN MEADOWLARK

BIGHORN SHEEP

OSPREY

RED FOX

PAINTBRUSH

COYOTE

MALLARD

BELTED KINGFISHER

WESTERN TOAD

MOUNTAIN BLUEBIRD

WILLOW FLYCATCHER

BEAVER

BISON

WILLOW

PRONGHORN ANTELOPE

COTTONWOOD

SNOWSHOE HARE

RED-TAILED HAWK

RAVEN

CANADA GOOSE

GOLDEN EAGLE

LITTLE BROWN BAT

GREAT HORNED OWL

ELK

BADGER

BLACK BEAR

RUFFED GROUSE

OTTER

MAGPIE

PURPLE ASTER

SILVERY BLUE MOTH

GOLDEN-MANTLED GROUND SQUIRREL

PINE MARTEN

CHIPMUNK

WHITE-TAILED JACKRABBIT

YELLOWSTONE CUTTHROAT TROUT

LONG-TAILED WEASEL

ARROWLEAF BALSAMROOT

RED SQUIRREL

LUPINE

MOUNTAIN CHICKADEE

GRIZZLY BEAR

RUFOUS HUMMINGBIRD

GOLDENROD

MOOSE

PORCUPINE

HERA BUCKMOTH

RED-WINGED BLACKBIRD

COLUMBIA SPOTTED FROG

DOWNY WOODPECKER

BOHEMIAN WAXWING

MILBERT'S TORTOISESHELL BUTTERFLY

COUGAR

SANDHILL CRANE

SAGEBRUSH

NORTHERN FLICKER

GOLDEN-CROWNED KINGLET

BALD EAGLE

YELLOW WARBLER

STICKY GERANIUM

GREAT BLUE HERON